The Power of Passion

By

Carl F. Hicks, Jr., Ph.D.

and

Natalya H. Bah, PMP, MSPM

ISBN: 1724495267
ISBN-13: 978-1724495266

High Impact Publishing, Chevy Chase, Maryland
www.HighImpactPublishing.com

Printed in the United States of America

The Power of Passion

Table of Contents

Introduction 9

1. Rediscovering Your Passion 15

2. Clarifying Your Passion 23

3. Optimizing Your Passion 33

Conclusion: Strengthening Your Passion . 43

About the Authors 50

Excerpts from the Power Series 61

The Power of Perspective Excerpt 63

The Power of Purpose Excerpt 71

The Power of Preparation Excerpt 79

The Power of Positivity Excerpt 87

The Power of Perseverance Excerpt 95

A Note from the Authors

Successful individuals in all walks of life often exhibit similar patterns of thinking and behaving. The authors believe it is helpful for those of you on a success journey to have the opportunity to read about and reflect upon these successful patterns of thinking and behaving that we have observed.

The authors have identified the Success Mindsets as Perspective, Purpose, and Passion and the Success Accelerators as Preparation, Positivity, and Perseverance. Each concise book in the series gives an overview of the topic identified. Additionally, each book provides questions to help you consider and increase your own level of these mindsets and accelerators.

Introduction

"Working hard for something we don't care about is called stress. Working hard for something we love is called passion."

–Simon Sinek,
Author, Motivational Speaker,

Passion is a powerful force. It is the major fuel for achieving our dreams and our goals. What is your passion? When was the last time you took inventory of your passions and considered whether you are living your life pursuing them? Passion is defined as a "strong liking or desire for or a devotion to some activity, object, or concept."[1]

1. "Passion." Merriam-Webster.com 2018.https://www.Merriam-Webster.com (7 March 2018)

The more passionate we are about something, the more likely it is that we will be successful at it. Think about people you've known who have been very passionate about their work. Doesn't it seem like they are the ones who receive the greatest notice and accolades? They live their devotion and are rewarded for it.

Without passion, life can become dull, stagnant. There might be ambition, but no momentum to move towards a goal.

Sometimes we get stuck at a place in our life's journey, and we need help in getting unstuck. It may be helpful to refine, clarify, and crystalize what we are truly passionate about. We cannot overemphasize the power of passion as a propellant to helping us fulfill our dreams.

This book will walk you through rediscovering your passion by providing questions to help you think deeply about your passions. We'll then clarify your passions by revisiting activities you greatly enjoyed as a child and how to use other factors to more deeply understand your passions.

Finally, we'll discuss why pursing your passion is important to becoming the "you," you were meant to be.

Do I make decisions in my life without considering my passions?

What are you passionate about?

What gets you up in the morning? What makes you jump out of bed? What makes you eager to get to the office, to start constructing a building, to lead a meeting, to teach a class, to sell a product, to perform a service, to bring joy to others?

Whatever your answer, I hope it has you "running" as fast as you can. I hope it lights your fire, fuels your energy, and propels you into your "zone of greatness." The "zone of greatness" is where your passion meets your unique talents. This is the intersection where the activities you love to do meet the activities you do so well.

We have all experienced this place. It goes by many names: the zone, the element, flow and flourish. Regardless of how we label it, it is a place where we can be fulfilled, where we can become all we are capable of becoming, where we can self-actualize, where we are the happiest.

It is the place we willingly run to—as quickly as we can. It is the place we willingly run to—as often as we can. It is the place we willingly run to—to be our best. It is the place we willingly run to—to be our true self.

Are you running as fast as you can toward your happiness?

Chapter One

Rediscovering Your Passion

"*Passion is energy. Feel the power that comes from focusing on what excites you.*"

- Oprah Winfrey,
Media Proprietor, Producer, Actress, Philanthropist

Sometimes people say, "I really don't know what I'm passionate about. Can you suggest ways to help me identify those activities I am most passionate about?" Many of us are interested in a lot of different types of activities. Some of us are interested in only one or two things, but almost all of us can identify with something that we are attracted to or energized by, excited about, or motivated by.

We believe that your core passions are already inside

of you. It's what you love to do. While you may be paid for certain work-related activities, that is not the primary reason you do them. It's what makes you feel good about yourself, and when engaged in these passionate activities, makes you lose all track of time. It's what you love to talk about with others. These are the true indications of your core passions. Focusing on your interests can be the starting point for identifying your passions.

Every great endeavor begins with passion.

There are several critical questions that we can ask ourselves to start to get a grasp on those activities that we are passionate about.

First, consider what you love to do. It may be helpful to consider activities that you enjoy participating in such as working in the garden, traveling, playing tennis or arranging flowers; or activities you do at work such as making presentations, creating schedules, or thinking strategically. Let your mind wander as far as you want. There are no restrictions. Think of as many enjoyable activities as you can.

For each of the activities you come up with, consider how each activity makes you feel. Whether they are work-related or play-related activities, do they make you feel happy, proud, or satisfied? Those items that evoke strong positive feelings are usually a pretty good indicator of your passion.

Again, when you're involved in these activities, does time seem to fly? If so, then that's another sign that the activity holds a special meaning for you. When you become so involved in an activity that you lose all sense of time, you can be certain that the activity is part of your being.

For the work activities you enjoy, do you enjoy them so much that you would do them for free? If the answer is yes, then that item is certainly a strong candidate for you to consider as a major passion.

Passion inspires dreams and provides the desire to bring them to life.

Another indication of a strong passion is that you love to talk about it. People who love an activity, goal, occupation, or profession just love to talk about it in a favorable or positive way.

Often, their excitement increases as they explain why they are so attracted to or motivated by the activity. They enjoy sharing their positive feelings.

The hope is that by considering these posibilites, you've formulated a strong initial picture of what you are passionate about.

What do you love to do?

Trust Your Heart

"The key is to trust your heart to move where your unique talents can flourish."
-Al Sacharov

Some years ago upon returning from Japan, I was asked if I had climbed Mount Fuji.

"No," I replied.

The follow up question was, "Why not?"

Although it was a simple question, I took my time formulating my response.

Perhaps the easiest way to explain why I never attempted to climb Mount Fuji was that I never had a passionate desire to do so.

The mountain was there. It was in sight. It could have been a worthwhile accomplishment.

Yet, I never even considered it.

Not having any passion about the task, I never formulated a goal, a plan, or a time frame. Therefore, I never climbed this famous mountain. In short, climbing Mount Fuji was not on my radar, nor was it in my heart.

What is in your heart? Is there something you want, or something want to do? What or who do you care about? Is there within you a compelling desire to move toward some positive activity?

Search your heart. Listen to your inner voice. There you will find your passion. And, when you do—follow it with zeal!

Chapter Two

Clarifying Your Passion

"The things you are passionate about are not random. They are your calling."

- Fabienne Frederickson,
Business Consultant, Entrepreneur, Author

In her book ***GRIT, The Power of Passion and Perseverance***, Angela Duckworth discusses how different our paths to discovering our passion can be. Some of us recognize our passions early in life and some late in life. In her book are examples of people having an immediate "a-ha" moment about their passion, and others having had a longer path to determining their true passion. In fact, she talks about the need to "foster a passion."

Regardless of whether you have a starting definition of your passion or are at a loss, it's always good to continue encouraging the development and growth of your passion. A starting point for doing this can be to remember what you were passionate about earlier in your life.

Reflecting upon your childhood activities may allow you to rediscover some activities that made you feel good about yourself. Look back on your childhood and try to see what fascinated you that might still fascinate you today. Consider recapturing those feelings and incorporating them into your life today.

Some might say, "Well, I don't really have any overriding interests. I enjoy a number of different things." In these cases, passion might be based more on general traits, unfolding over time.

Others might say, "Well, you know I really like helping people. I'm never quite sure what that means in terms of operationalizing it, but I've enjoyed doing it." This is a good starting point for delving deeper into those more general traits and considering them from a new viewpoint. For instance, what are the traits you enjoy using the most?

Passion breathes life into natural talent, giving it purpose and meaning.

Sometimes our passions come out in the friendships that we form as an adult, the types of conversations that exhilarate us, or the experiences that we create for ourselves.

I had a client named Lisa who had been a very successful seller of insurance for many years. Her sales income had plateaued, and we were working together to determine how she could turn that around. I urged her to take some time to reflect on what she was passionate about. After a bit of consideration, she realized it was her mother.

That discovery evolved into her setting aside 10% of one of her income streams to save for a big trip with her mother. She developed such an excitement for the trip that by the time they went, she had earned enough for two trips. Her passion for traveling with her mother drove her professional success.

You can also consider weekends or vacations—what do you do then that you would not normally do during the week?

It could be hiking, or swimming, or other physical activities. Think about what you do that nobody is making you do, or that you're doing solely because it is fun.

Passion makes the ordinary extraordinary.

Sometimes we can take that passion and make it a career. For instance, I know a lawyer for a government agency who came home each day and went into his home art studio. He created beautiful portraits and was most animated when talking about his art. Eventually he made the transition from attorney to full-time artist. He lives his passion every day.

At it's most basic level, discovering your passion comes down to one, simple question: what do you love to do? The answer will help you clarify what your passion is and how to begin pursuing it.

Passion breathes life into the stagnant and transforms the dull into something dazzling.

What did you love as a child?

Stay Alive

"On life's vast ocean diversely we sail.
Reason the card, passion the gale.'"
- Alexander Pope

The drowning person struggles to stay afloat, struggles for air. During those moments, all other thoughts and concerns are irrelevant. The drowning person is passionate about one thing: surviving the ordeal.

Every day we encounter many distractions, distractions that take our focus off of our most important tasks. Sure, we can make our list of things to do. Sure, we can write our goals on our "vision board." Sure, we can list our reasons why on our "Magic Clouds."

What's missing? Passion!

It is our deep-seated passion to go somewhere, be someone, do something important, and achieve a critical objective that fuels our activities.

It is the passion to live that propels the drowning person to tread water. It is the passion to live that propels the drowning person to gasp for air. If this passion dissipates, the result is a lost life.

Do you have the passion to live?

Chapter Three

Optimizing Your Passion

"*You have to be burning with an idea or a problem or a wrong that you want to right. If you're not passionate enough from the start, you will never stick it out.*"

– Steve Jobs,
American Entreprenuer, Business Magnate

Now that we've delved deeper into your passions, we want to use that information to think about how to live a life that's significant, fulfilling for you, and makes you feel better about how you're using your talents. Your passion is the fuel that makes you lose track of time and helps you feel good about yourself. It also helps you enjoy doing an activity to the best of your ability, particularly those activities that you might be exceptional at. For that reason, passion is the driving force that directs our lives. The question is, are you utilizing your passion to make sure you are excelling?

Talent and drive are only part of the force behind achievement. The rest is passion.

If you're not excited about what you're doing, if you're not excited about your dreams, if you're not excited about the way you're living your life, it will be difficult for other people to get excited for you. Yes, you can seek help from coaches and mentors and others that you respect to help you in sharpening your vision of your passions, but the answers are within you.

Each person is unique. When you combine what you love to do (your passions) and what you do exceedingly well (your peak performance), you have identified your unique abilities. Your unique abilities can be both "play" related and "work" related.

Your unique abilities, as defined above, make up your uniqueness. It's what makes you *you.* This is your zone of greatness—where you will feel that you are doing, and being, and becoming all that you were meant to be.

Knowing your passion gives you something to build the rest of your life around. Your passion can be almost anything if it challenges you, intrigues you, motivates you, and brings you a sense of fulfillment and happiness. When we work hard at something we love to do, it doesn't really seem like work, because it is fulfilling.

It is important that you make sure you are optimizing your passion. Are you investing your time and energy in those activities that make the most of your core passions?

One starting point is to ask yourself whether you are spending your time the way you really want to be spending your time. If money were no object, would you be doing what you're doing now? You can also examine if there are specific parts of your job that you would rather not do.

Passion gives a sense of excitement and joy to the hard work of cultivating talent and interest.

Another important question is, what would you attempt to do if you knew you could not fail? This is really another simple question to help determine whether you are on the right passion path.

Suppose you say, "Well, I'd like to be a world-famous singer." Think about this for a moment. Is this something you have the talent to do?

The level of talent doesn't always determine the level of success. There are many world-famous singers who have less talent than other singers who are less well-known. Ask yourself: are these less-talented singers more successful because of their passion?

Another interesting question to ask yourself is, who would you like to switch places with? Remember that this has to be a person who is currently alive. What is it about their life that makes you want to switch places with them? Consider what you value about that person, what they contribute, and what they are passionate about.

Now, combine your answer to the questions above with the passions you have rediscovered and clarified earlier in this book. Take an honest look at your life and analyze whether you are you living a life that is full of what you are passionate about. Are you utilizing the strength of your passions to lead the most successful life possible?

If your answer to these questions is no, what can you do about it? Consider what actions you can take to ensure that your passions become a more significant part of your life. Perhaps you should commit to specific steps such as taking inventory of your passions on a regular basis or considering your passions before making decisions. Or, like the lawyer/artist mentioned earlier, maybe you need to make more significant changes in your life. Whatever you decide, a life filled with passion is going to result in one that is more joyful and successful.

Are you living a life that fully incorporates your passion?

Which path will you chose?

"Stop chasing the money and start chasing the passion."'"

-Winston Churchill,

It is very easy to equate success with numbers and assets, but as the saying goes, money can't buy happiness.

The signs of success—money, fame, power, possessions—will never satisfy, because meaningful success is not defined by these things. A true sense of success comes when you have fulfilled your passion, which, in turn, leads to the fulfillment of your purpose.

The crafting and pursuit of passion gives hard work and determination true meaning. When you are striving toward a goal that aligns with your passion, the work will be more productive and more significant than a goal that is aligned with your possessions.

The opportunity for growth, fulfillment, and

and purpose comes on the path that is paved with passion. Which path will you chose?

Conclusion

Strengthening Your Passion

"It is the soul's duty to be loyal to its own desires. It must abandon itself to its master passion."

– Rebecca West,
Author, Journalist, Literary Critic

Passion is the fuel that can propel us toward the realization of our dreams. Passion helps us get started on our Greatness Journey and keeps us moving through tough times. When fully engaged in a pursuit we love, passion sets us on fire. It excites us.

People who are passionate display it. You can see the excitement in their eyes, the enthusiasm in their voice, the smile on their face, or the bounce in their step.

To get to this point with our own passion, we need to spend time rediscovering and clarifying our passions. This process allows us to first reevaluate our passions to understand what we really love. Digging deeper by considering past passions and other factors allows us to gain an even clearer picture of our passions.

Don't settle for ordinary. Unleash your passion . . . and prepare for *extraordinary.*

But we cannot stop there, we also need to consider whether we are living our life full of our passions. If we can optimize the passions in our life, we can live a more satisfying and successful life. To refer back to the Rebecca West quote, this requires us listening to our master passion.

Who can you talk to—a friend, family member, or colleague—to help keep your passions at the forefront of your life?

The Power of Passion

Every great endeavor begins with passion. Whether it's personal or professional, passion is the motivational force behind the venture. It is the energy behind the forward motion.

Without passion, life can become dull, stagnant. There might be ambition, but no momentum to move towards the goal.

Passion, however, not only provides the energy needed to move forward, it provides a sense of meaning and purpose to even the smallest of pursuits. Passion breathes life into the stagnant and transforms the dull into something dazzling.

Are you harnessing the power of passion?

The Power of Passion

About the Authors

Carl F. Hicks, Jr., consults with successful senior executives and business owners who want more. More personal and professional growth. More productivity and profitability. More meaning and happiness. More quality thinking time.

As President/CEO of The Growth Group, LLC, Carl works with some of America's best-managed companies helping them to identify and develop their top managerial talent, strengthen their work teams, and optimize their organization's performance.

Through his conversational-coaching approach, Carl keeps clients actively engaged and focused on critical strategic initiatives, growth, and profitability - while maintaining a balance between their Life Style Goals, their Livelihood Goals, and their Quarterly Strategic Initiatives.

Clients range from emerging entrepreneurs to Fortune 100 firms. His results-oriented approach to management combines a formal education—Ph.D. in Business Administration and MBA from The University of Arkansas and B.S. in Management with Distinction from Mississippi State University — with more than thirty years of practical consulting experience.

Carl is on the Board of Directors of Lifetime Financial Growth, LLC, and has been recognized by Birkman International as a Birkman Master Certified Professional, a designation earned by only 5% of their consultants worldwide. Carl is also an active member of Forbes Coaches Council.

Carl and his wife, Carolyn, have a daughter, Natalya, and son-in-law, Mahmoud, who have blessed them with three wonderful grandchildren. Carl and Carolyn share their homes in Chevy Chase, Maryland, and Hilton Head Island, South Carolina, with Delta, their beloved Maltese.

Natalya H. Bah helps individuals and organizations alike define and achieve their goals. With services such as team building, executive coaching, and in-person and online training, she caters to a wide variety of interests and needs. The clients of Natalya H. Bah Consulting come from many fields ranging from legal, financial services, and real estate, to government and non-profit.

As a certified Birkman Method© consultant, Natalya utilizes the highly effective self-assessment program, along with other activities and exercises, to foster team building and strengthening in her clients. Past sessions have specifically focused on increasing effective communication, preparing for organizational change, increasing employee engagement, and understanding and meeting motivational drivers.

For her executive coaching services, Natalya created the Define and Achieve Your Goals Process™, which includes companion workbooks and online courses such as "Getting Goal Ready." This process is available for both individuals and groups.

In addition to the courses she offers online, Natalya creates and delivers in-person training on project management and leadership. She has used her training services to help organizations develop leaders, improve their project success rate, and meet their strategic goals.

Natalya has spoken at a variety of conferences and symposiums. With a relaxed, interactive facilitation style, she speaks to groups of all sizes on a wide range of topics including goal-setting and achievement, project management, self-assessments, employee engagement, and change management.

Having received her Master of Science degree in Project Management from George Washington University's School of Business, Natalya is also a certified Project Management Professional (PMP). She lives in Bethesda, Maryland, with her husband, Mahmoud, and their three children.

Also Available by Carl F. Hicks, Jr. and Natalya H. Bah

The Power of Perspective

By

Carl F. Hicks, Jr.

and

Natalya H. Bah

Are you living the life you want to live? A life of purpose? Of meaning? Are you on your way to reaching the level of success you believe you're capable of? If not, it's time to harness the Power of Perspective.

The Power of Purpose

By

Carl F. Hicks, Jr.

and

Natalya H. Bah

Discovering your purpose is in life is like finding the missing piece of a puzzle: all the other pieces make sense, and the meaning becomes clear. Have you harnessed the Power of Purpose?

Available by Carl F. Hicks, Jr.

The Best You

By

Carl F. Hicks, Jr.

A collection of motivational quotes by Carl to help spark a thoughtful assessment of where you are now, and inspire a vision of where you'd like to go.

Unlock the Growth Potential of Your Organization
By
Carl F. Hicks, Jr., Ph.D. and
Martin E. Willoughby, Jr., J.D.

With this innovative tool, learn how to understand and motivate each individual in your organization in order to achieve collective success.

Available now at Amazon.com and
Barnes&Noble.com

Are you ready for a Hicks Fix?

Visit **TheHicksFix.com** today!

Learn more about The Growth Group, LLC, awareness and growth enhancing services:

- Executive Coaching
- Team Strengthening
- Organizational Optimization

Discover valuable resources:

- Monthly High Impact Ideas and Coaching Tips
- Podcasts
- Worksheets
- Videos

THE GROWTH GROUP
Consultants to Management

Read on for excerpts from the Power Series:

The Power of Perspective

The Power of Purpose

The Power of Preparation

The Power of Positivity

The Power of Perseverance

The Power of Perspective

By

Carl F. Hicks, Jr., Ph.D.

and

Natalya H. Bah, PMP, MSPM

Excerpt

The Power of Perspective

"A change in your perspective can result in a seismic shift in your life."

–Natalya H. Bah, Co-Author

Art loved the view from his second story balcony. From that perch, he could enjoy the daily sunsets over the Pacific Ocean. He found the fading colors invigorating. His colleague Dave, on the other hand, could never see nor appreciate the sunset from his basement apartment.

Sometimes Art and Dave would have the opportunity to work together on the same project. Both were equally skilled and talented and had graduated from top universities. Yet Art and Dave's perspectives of what was possible were as different as their views from their apartments. Art had an expanding perspective and was never deterred when issues or obstacles arose. Dave, on the other hand, had a confining perspective. Dave would get frustrated by unexpected changes and saw them as barriers, not opportunities to do things better.

Art's perspective on life tended to reflect his "balcony" view. With that perspective, Art continued to grow and develop and eventually moved into his dream job. His career advancement was enhanced by his "balcony" view.

Our perspective determines how successful we'll be in our work and life. It influences how we think and see the world and how we interact with people and react to events. Successful individuals have a perspective that tends to drive them toward successful outcomes. They tend to see opportunities in problems. They look on the bright side of things and visualize results.

As you read this book, we invite you to examine and reflect upon your perspective. When was the last time that you really considered what your perspective was, and how it might be affecting your life? How does your perspective affect how you see and react to situations in your life and career? How in control of your perspective are you?

Perspective is a powerful word. It's defined by Merriam Webster as providing "the ability to understand what is important and what isn't."[1] Would you benefit from the

1. "Perspective." Merriam-Webster.com 2018.https:/rwww.Merriam-Webster.com (7 March 2018)

opportunity to consider what is important in your life, and how you can harness this powerful tool to make you more succussful?

Throughout this book, we will provide you with questions that will help you investigate and strengthen your perspective. We hope you'll allow your perspective—hopefully from the balcony and not the basement—to drive you toward personal and professional success.

A Moment of Perspective . . .

How is your vision?

Some people view the world through the lens of rose-colored glasses. Others see the world through "woe-shaded" glasses.

But there are some who choose to wear "vision" glasses and "see" what's not there . . . but could be.

- *They see an opportunity, where others may see a problem.*
- *They see a future, where others may be stuck in the past.*
- *They envision greatness, while others experience envy or fear.*

So, how is your vision? Is it time for an eye exam?

The Power of Purpose

By

Carl F. Hicks, Jr., Ph.D.

and

Natalya H. Bah, PMP, MSPM

Excerpt

The Power of Purpose

"There are two great days in a person's life—the day we are born and the day we discover why."

–William Barclay, Author, Scholar

Knowing your *why*—your purpose—is a powerful success mindset. Typically, people can tell you what they do for a living, and how they do it, but some struggle with explaining "why" they do what they do for a living.

So why is it important to know your "why," your purpose for doing what you do? Strong determination from the inside enhances what a person is trying to do, be, or become. A clear, internal purpose can channel your energy, provide fuel for your efforts, and keep you focused on your intentions. Once you identify your purpose, you can focus on a more intentional effort toward a goal you want to accomplish. If there's no clear purpose, you may drift off course.

Purpose transforms activity into achievement.

Purpose is defined as "the reason for which something exists or is done, made, used, etc."[1] Your reason helps you shape your vision and propels you toward your initiative or goal. When you encounter adversity, your reason helps you move forward anyway.

People who have a clear grasp of their why—and we equate that with the word "purpose"—can be truly intentional in their efforts. Your purpose comes from your values, beliefs, passions, and what you determine is important to you. It comes from knowing that you have certain talents and from

1. "Purpose." Learners Dictionary.com 2018.https://www.learnersdictionary.com

visualizing the results you desire. Once you have taken ownership of your purpose, no one can take it away from you.

With purpose, you can focus more on how you want to live your life—and maybe even how you want to be remembered—as opposed to only what you have accomplished. We all have purpose inside of us, but we have to nurture and shape it. You'll have to surface and enhance your purpose before it can give meaning to your life.

Do You Know Where You're Going?

Cat: "Where are you going?"

Alice: "Which way should I go?"

Cat: "That depends on where you are going?"

Alice: "I don't know."

Cat: "Then it doesn't matter which way you go."

-Lewis Carroll, ***Alice in Wonderland***

In Lewis Carroll's classic ***Alice in Wonderland****, Alice did not have a compelling "purpose" to propel her toward a desirable destination. She may eventually arrive "some place," but is it the "some place" she wanted to be? Or will she just fit herself into the "some place" she has reached?*

Some people have such a strong purpose that they are motivated to endure all kinds of hardships to reach their desired destination. Their strong purpose provides both a sense of direction and motivation to pursue a specific course of action. They will not settle for less.

Others have only a vague notion of what they want or where they are going. They become discouraged at the first obstacle. The lack of a definitive purpose provides little sense of direction and limited motivation. They will likely be tempted to settle for anything.

The Power of Preparation

By

Carl F. Hicks, Jr., Ph.D.

and

Natalya H. Bah, PMP, MSPM

Excerpt

The Power of Preparation

"There are other players who were more talented, but there is no one who could out-prepare me."

–Peyton Manning
Two-Time Super Bowl Champion
Five -Time National Football League Most Valuable Player

***Semper Paratus* –United States Coast Guard Motto**

Continuous preparation is a hallmark of champions, and a strong perspective can be enhanced by intentional, purposeful, determined, definitive, and disciplined preparation. Being fully prepared occurs one step at a time, and preparation can be conceptualized as the build-up of useful skill sets over time.

Each of us needs to ask ourselves, "What skills do I need to ensure success?" and "What do I need to know how to do exceedingly well to be *Semper Paratus*—always ready?"

Intentional and purposeful preparation suggests that one devote considerable thought to the *why* and *what* of the planned preparation. Are you wanting to improve an already established skill? Do you want to strengthen a skill that has the potential for further development? The most likely response will be a "yes" to both questions.

Peyton Manning spent countless hours reviewing game film, notes by scouts, and his own thoughts in preparation for each game. He once said that he may not have been the most skilled player on the field, but he was the most prepared. A blog post by Sport Psychology Quotes (July 21, 2011) quoted Manning describing his consistent preparation:

> "In the NFL game today, there are a lot of better athletes than I am, and quarterbacks these days are faster than the quarterbacks have always been,

they're running like crazy. But I kind of stick to my roots of the disciplined quarterback. You know, I'm doing the same routine every week, studying tapes and working hard, getting ready to play and making good decisions on Sunday."

The thoroughness of Manning's preparation manifested itself in wins, MVP awards, and a number of other individual and team NFL records. In his final game as a professional football player, his team won the 2016 Super Bowl. Peyton credited his intense preparation as a contributing factor to his confidence.

Dr. Denton Cooley, the noted heart surgeon, completed the first successful heart transplant in the United States and performed more than 120,000 open heart operations during his career. He had great manual dexterity and surgical efficiency. Other surgeons commented on his lightning speed, the huge volume of daily surgeries, and his "Tiffany-level" quality. Surgeons came to Houston from all over the world to observe his procedures.

Dr. Christian Barnard said, "It was the most beautiful surgery I had ever seen. No one could equal it. Dr. Cooley's skill was matched by his grace and kindness."

His surgical procedures were focused, decisive, efficient, and effective—all outcomes of his intentional and purposeful preparation. One example of his purposeful practice involved tying knots inside of a small box as preparation for efficiently tying off surgical sutures in the confined space of a patient's chest cavity.

Champions such as Peyton Manning and Dr. Denton Cooley were able to reach the highest levels of achievement in their respective fields through dedication, hard work, and purposeful preparation. They were fortunate to have been in a calling where what they loved to do and what they did well came together.

Some may say that they were lucky. Luck may play a role, but their success did not happen by chance. Their 'luck' was the result of their preparation meeting with opportunities presented to them. "Luck is what happens when preparation meets opportunity," claimed Seneca.

The question of what to prepare for finds its response in the clarity of one's perspective. Preparation is enhanced by the clarity of your perspective. As you gain clarity about how you see the world, what you want from it, and what you are willing to do to get what you want, the preparation necessary becomes clear.

The Power of Positivity

By

Carl F. Hicks, Jr., Ph.D.

and

Natalya H. Bah, PMP, MSPM

Excerpt

The Power of Positivity

"If you think you can do a thing or think you can't do a thing, you're right."

–Henry Ford
Founder of Ford Motor Company

If you think you can change your way of living by changing your way of thinking, and you take action, then we believe you can. However, if you think that you can't change your life for the better, and you don't even try, then you won't. How we see a situation or an event or respond to people's words depends upon how we think about where we are, who we are, and what we can do. In short, how we *think* influences our lives and actions.

"I can do this!"

Several years ago, when one of our granddaughters was about six years old, my wife and I (Carl) took her to a birthday party at a bowling alley. I hadn't been in a bowling alley in a long time and I wondered, "How are these children going to be able to lift the bowling ball and throw it down the lane?"

What I found out was that the alley adds a bumper for children to prevent gutter balls. If the child can toss or drop the bowling ball, it'll roll down the alley. With the bumper, it'll continue down the lane and most likely hit some pins.

Two children, in particular, caught my attention with their different approaches to the game. The first was a three-foot girl who weighed about 30 pounds. Each time it was her turn, she'd become excited, jump around, and say, "I can do this. I can do this. I can do this."

She'd grab a bowling ball and struggle up to the line and drop the ball. She obviously couldn't throw it, because it was too heavy. Although she could barely make it up to the line, she'd drop the ball and then start jumping and yelling, "Strike! Strike! Strike!"

The ball rolled slowly, yet it would knock some pins down with the assistance of the bumpers. I noticed that she actually made two strikes. It was always exciting to watch her jump up and down and yell, "Strike! Strike! Strike!" every time she bowled.

In contrast, a four-foot boy weighing about 15-20 pounds more than the girl would complain about the weight of the ball and how hard it was to bowl. His hunched shoulders revealed his reluctance as he walked up to the line. He was bigger and had more strength than the girl, so he should have been able to put more force behind the ball before throwing it down the alley. After he threw the ball, however, I noticed he would turn to his left and walk away with his head down and a dejected look on his face. He would say, "This is too difficult. The ball is too heavy, and the pins are too far away."

Almost every time, the ball would move to the left and ride down the bumper. It would hit just one or two pins. I never saw him get a strike.

Locus of Control

As I watched these two children bowl, it dawned on me that the young girl who was approaching this activity in a positive manner had what we call an internal locus of control.

Locus is another word for location. People who have an internal locus of control about a certain event or activity in their life believe that they can exert some impact on the result that might occur. Her jumping up and down and yelling, "Strike! Strike! Strike!" indicated that she believed that she could do it, and on a couple of occasions she actually did.

The opposite of internal locus of control is what's referred to as an external locus of control. This refers to a belief that one can't change an outcome no matter what actions are taken, and that one's results are beyond one's control.

Our loci of control varies depending upon the situation or task. For example, the very next day the young man may have had an internal locus of control as he was out on the soccer field, and the young woman may have had an external locus of control as she was at art class. We're always somewhere on that continuum.

The Power of Perseverance

By

Carl F. Hicks, Jr., Ph.D.

and

Natalya H. Bah, PMP, MSPM

Excerpt

The Power of Perseverance

"On the steep slope of success can be found the victorious who are determined to persevere and to reach their dreams."

–Carl F. Hicks, Jr., Co-Author

After eighteen years of trying, Sergio Garcia won the Masters on Sunday, April 9, 2017, in his 74th attempt at winning a major golf title. He began his journey in 1999 when he first captivated golf fans at the PGA Championship. Over the years, he encountered one disappointment after another with losses and close wins. Garcia persevered through hardships and frustration and teaches us all to never give up. He's considered a true champion—not just because he won—but because he never gave up on his dream.

Success stories have three major parts: the beginning, middle, and end. In measuring success, we often focus on the difference between the start of our success journey and the completion or results achieved. The middle part, the route between start and finish, can contain ups and downs, starts and stops, and zigs and zags. It's rarely a straight line. The middle part of success can be a mixed bag.

It's in this middle part when you may start to experience obstacles. Situations can become complex and people frustrating. Sometimes, it may seem that the harder you work, the further behind you get, or you may feel trapped by circumstances beyond your control. Negative emotions can start to dominate your thinking and affect your behavior. You may entertain the idea of quitting.

It is precisely at this time that you will

need to dig deep inside of yourself and pull up all of your perseverance reserves.

I like to define perseverance as the ability to steadfastly stay the course in the pursuit of a goal, task, dream or journey, regardless of the difficulties, distractions, or obstacles faced, or the frustration and discouragement experienced. What do you think of when you hear the word perseverance? When was the last time to considered how your ability to persevere impacts your life?

Printed in Dunstable, United Kingdom

77236434R00060